*"**DANGER:** Reading this book can be hazardous to your habit of procrastination.* *Stop Procrastinating Now* describes a wonderfully practical and effective process that can help busy people regain control of their lives. Kerul's approach is refreshingly counter-intuitive yet simple, and will help you get the important things done. After all, struggle is strictly overrated."

> – Kim George, founder and CEO of The AQ Institute and
> bestselling author of *Coaching Into Greatness:*
> *4 Steps to Success in Business and Life*

"Kerul, I was informed, enlightened and even entertained by your book. Of particular interest to me were the real-life stories about creative ways to overcome procrastination (like the client who had to pay you an extra $50 if she didn't get her writing done!) I also saw myself in the description of the "anticrastinator"–the person who rushes to get things completed and doesn't really enjoy the process. Full of practical strategies and wise insights, this book is a valuable resource for anyone who wants to overcome procrastination."

> – Barbra Sundquist, AC-CC, CVCC,
> Certified Mentor Coach

"Kerul took me right through the murky maze of what makes us procrastinate. I find that hiring the 'hit man' to assist me in dropping my "old goals" made so much sense! An over-investment in my old goals was really holding me back from moving ahead and ahead is where I wished I was. Now that I have arrived, I'll keep my 'hit man' with me, a good and trusted 'friend'. Thanks Kerul."

> – Patricia J. Foley, CPA

"What a gift! I think I've been putting off overcoming procrastination just waiting for this amazing book! SO full of practical techniques, SO bursting with wisdom and SO much fun to read. I'm always a bit skeptical when reading a "solution" in a book but this one is the real deal. Thank you for giving me a whole new way of looking at how I get things done... I am already much more productive as a result of the techniques in this book."

– Maria E. Andreu, Marketing Solutions Consultant

"Kerul's *Five Radical Procrastination Strategies* is sure to get you out of your head, and into action. I particularly enjoyed the helpful (and often entertaining) real-life examples woven throughout the book. Good stuff!"

– Kathy Gulrich, Marketing & Product Development Coach

"It is an easy read with practical, useful strategies. The real-life examples that are weaved in really help to illustrate the concepts at work."

– Gina Pastella, Boardman, Ohio

"Thank you so much for your wonderful book, *5 Radical Procrastination Strategies*. I loved it! I saw your humor and your in-depth understanding of procrastination in every section. More importantly, I saw myself (or at least bits of myself) all through it. While I consider myself a pretty action-oriented person and very disciplined, I still saw ways that I could make the process of 'getting things done' much more enjoyable. I also learned that I have tendencies to be an "anticrastinator" and that may not be the virtuous asset that I've tried to convince myself it is (in fact, I see how some of my challenges have come from anticrastination.) The book is chock full of information—I will certainly read it a several more times to be sure that I've gotten all of the nuggets that I need from it!"

– Judy Toth, M.S., Personal Effectiveness Coach

"I have read many books and articles on procrastination and have even delivered workshops on the topic but am still struggling with "never getting around" to certain tasks. What really jumped out in Kerul's article is her statement "Intention without action is like a car without wheels; you may have a vehicle but it's really hard to get around. WOW!!! I am going to print this in large letters and post it all over my home to remind me that intentions are only the first part. If I want to achieve my goals, I have to put my intentions into action."

    – Francesca Riley, Licensed Third Age Coach, Montreal, Canada

"Consistently, Kerul's thoughts are insightful and provocative. She will de-bunk your perpetual patterns. So prepare to have some of your conventional thinking challenged in a way that you will grow to better understand your own way of operating."

    – Sarah K. Dolliver, Personal and business coach

"Kerul's book reflects her deep insight and expertise in the field of procrastination. Through the many examples shared, readers are awakened to many thoughts and inner obstacles which may stand in the way of their goal attainment. She gives excellent advice, and concrete methods for moving past procrastination. Before reading this ebook, I was unaware of all the ways I was blocking my own success. I highly recommend this book to anyone who has a goal or a dream they wish to move forward with."

    – Lynn Cohen, Personal and Professional Coach

"I was absolutely intrigued by this book. It exposes the hidden underbelly of why we don't accomplish our goals — and offers clear, hard-hitting strategies to fit different personalities and situations. For example, using Kerul's "hitman" strategy, I promoted a new coaching program before the program was developed. That was the perfect motivation to stop procrastinating and move into action!"

    – Patricia Soldati, Corporate Exit coach

Stop Procrastinating Now:

Five Radical Procrastination Strategies to Set You Free

By Kerul Kassel

Stop Procrastinating Now:

Five Radical Procrastination Strategies to Set You Free

By Kerul Kassel

New Leaf Publishing
PO Box 701379, St. Cloud, FL 34770

New Leaf Publishing
PO Box 701379
St. Cloud, FL 34770

ISBN 978-0-9786885-0-9

First New Leaf Publishing printing
January 2007

Printed in the U.S.A.

Contents

Strategy 3:
Hire a Hit Man to Kill You if
You Don't Follow Through

Strategy 4:
Don't Take Yes For an Answer

Strategy 5:
Stop Trying to Finish

Final Thoughts

Acknowledgements

My everlasting and heartfelt gratitude to goes out to the many people who helped me take this book from just a notion all the way to print. If you've ever written and published a book, you know how long and arduous the process can be!

To my husband Dave, my deepest appreciation for teaching me that immediate action isn't always intelligent, and especially for his patience, support, and love while I built my business and skills.

To Maria Andreu, for her invaluable help and fortitude in helping me to make sense of seemingly inscrutable marketing and Internet strategies, and for her ongoing championing of me.

To my clients for their courage and confidence, for providing so many stories, and for being my inspiration.

To my many teachers for challenging me, offering perspective, and helping to equip me with the most effective tools available.

To my respected and august colleagues for giving me feedback and encouragement throughout the development of this book.

And to all you readers, for your dedication to your own improvement, your open minds, and your willingness to experiment with radical strategies. Without you, this book would still be just an idea.

Introduction

Congratulations on taking a strong and positive step toward ending procrastination! I've worked with hundreds of clients and workshop participants over the last seven years. During that time, I've continued to hone and refine my approach and techniques. Most approaches to procrastination lack inspiration and are unlikely to have long-lasting effects. That's because they address the symptoms and not the roots of the problem.

In this book I'm defining procrastination as the act of putting something off when you know you're going to be worse off for having done so. I'm assuming you've thought about the negative consequences you could suffer for delaying.

I don't believe that procrastination is always a bad thing. Sometimes it's the best time management tool available – provided that the cost of procrastination is lower than the cost of getting things done. But most people don't use procrastination wisely, and the ideas in this book are designed to help overcome procrastination where it hurts, and use it skillfully when it's appropriate.

Procrastination is something you've probably been doing for years, perhaps decades. There are a lot of patterns and behaviors behind your procrastination, most of which you may not be aware of. Being successful at stopping procrastination hinges on becoming aware of those patterns and behaviors. That's what this book is about.

Don't look for immediate, complete, forever-changed habits everywhere across your life. That kind of expectation is unrealistic and sets you up for failure. What you're about to read offers you a new perspective and viable strategies to set you free you from much of what causes procrastination. But new habits are – habits, after all. And changing your habits takes time and repetition. Without a doubt, "life" will intrude here or there and push you off course – that's normal!

When that happens, don't fret and judge yourself and stop trying. Those are the types of attitudes I want to ask you to let go of.

If what you've tried so far hasn't worked, it's time for something new, and it's time to give that new approach an opportunity to work before you dismiss it.

I want you to get the most out of this book, so I'm going to ask you to do something right away – put your skepticism on hold while you read this book, and give the ideas a whirl. If you find yourself saying "But..." while you read, perhaps you're not used to such novel ideas, or maybe you're not as ready for change as you think.

Everything you read in this book has been developed and tested through years of work and thousands of hours with clients and workshop participants and through designing and delivering classes, and training other coaches in how to use some of the ideas in this book.

What you find here doesn't require hard work. Thank goodness, right?! That's the last thing you need in addition to what you already have to do. No, dear reader, all you need to do is try some new ideas and play with them, to see how they could work for you. This is probably quite different than what you've been taught, but that's a good thing.

You may want to start by taking the Procrastinator Profiler Quiz at the beginning of this book, especially if you haven't already taken it, since it's referred to within the content of the book. You'll find the quiz on page 1, or you can go to **www.newleafsystems.com/one.php** and get your results via email.

If you find that these ideas help you to make good start, but you're still not where you'd like to be, you may need more personalized attention so that you can say goodbye to procrastination. If so, please email me at **kerul@newleafsystems.com**, or go to my website at **www.newleafsystems.com** and check out the services and programs I offer.

I wish you much success in getting what you want, and never feeling ashamed of procrastinating again.

Kerul

The Procrastinator Profiler©

How many procrastinators does it take to finish a long quiz? None, they'll do it later! That's why this assessment is short and sweet.

If you're like most people, you're no stranger to procrastination. Some people procrastinate only on occasion or with particular tasks, and others hardly do it at all. Then there are the rest (most!) of us who put quite a few things off frequently.

The following quiz will help you to discover your Procrastinator Profile© and will give you key insights and proven strategies based on your answers. You may fit into more than one profile, and that's okay. It just means that you're on your way to the next level, closer to eliminating your procrastination.

For some questions, you may not find any answers that apply. Pick the one that's closest, or just skip the question. If none of the answers to any questions really apply to you, it could mean that you're really not a procrastinator after all!

1. In the past, when I've created an early deadline to try to get things done on time, I've:

   a. Forgotten to write the deadline down.

   b. Ignored the deadline to the best of my ability.

   c. Not realized it would take me longer than I planned.

   d. Not thought to plan what I needed to do.

   e. Yikes! All of the above.

f. Am usually successful at completing it on time.

2. About today's to-do list:

   a. I haven't looked at my to-do list yet.

   b. To-do lists are for anal retentive people.

   c. I can't possibly do everything on it today.

   d. I don't have a to-do list.

   e. I get overwhelmed and want to take a nap.

   f. I fully expect to get everything done.

3. I've tried to control or manage procrastination by:

   a. Telling myself I'll be better next time.

   b. Blaming circumstances or other people for it.

c. Saying I'll have to forego something nice, but I never make myself do it.

d. Controlling it? Hmm, that seems like it could be a good idea.

e. I'll never be successful at controlling it, that's just how I am.

f. Various methods that usually work.

4. When I catch myself in procrastination mode, I usually:

a. Think I'll do it later.

b. Don't want to be bothered because there are other things I'd like to do.

c. Am in the midst of working on something else that's productive.

d. Don't catch myself. Only later do I realize that I was procrastinating.

e. Feel kind of hopeless.

f. Don't really find myself in procrastination mode.

5. My incomplete projects are:

   a. On my to-do list, and have been for long time.

   b. Annoying!

   c. In my plans, but I haven't taken the next steps yet.

   d. Sitting around waiting to be finished some day.

   e. Countless, and depressing to think about.

   f. Not important enough to spend time on at the moment.

6. The kinds of things I put off in which someone else is affected:

   a. I almost always get done, even if it's right at the deadline.

   b. I sometimes get done, depending on how badly it'll affect me if I don't.

   c. Have made a lot of people mad at me.

7. The sorts of tasks I usually drag my feet on are:

    a. The details. I usually do the important stuff.

    b. Challenging or difficult.

    c. Just about anything tedious, boring, hard, or unpleasant.

8. Due to procrastination, my financial situation is:

    a. Not really affected by procrastination.

    b. Not terrible, but far from where it should be.

    c. Really shaky.

9. Because I've missed deadlines, forgotten or delayed completion of responsibilities at home or at work:

    a. I've had one or two confrontations with my boss, customers, significant other, or roommate.

b. There's often a lot of tension or arguments.

c. It's possible I might lose my job, my business, my marriage, or my friends.

10. Due to the stress of what I need to get done and haven't, I'm usually:

a. Productive and finishing most of what I want to accomplish.

b. A little edgy and tense.

c. Anxious, upset, and troubled.

11. I haven't been able to find a sustainable way to address my medical, nutritional, or fitness needs. As a result, my health:

a. Is not negatively affected much at all, fortunately!

b. Could definitely use improvement.

c. Isn't good and causes me to procrastinate even more.

Scoring

For questions 1–5. Count the number of each a, b, c, d and e answer. Whichever letter you picked most often is your procrastination profile.

A = The Unplanned Procrastinator:

You just lack a follow-through plan, a simple system or process to take concerted or consistent action. You've thought about how to get things done, and have had some good ideas, but you just haven't put them into place yet. It's probable that you have too much on your to-do list, and it's time to weed out unnecessary tasks by creating a "not-to-do" list! Spend just a few minutes each day to review what you really need to get done, and make a plan of action that you refer to once or twice later during the day. This is one of the best ways to make things happen. If you've had trouble prioritizing or have been unsuccessful so far, it doesn't mean you're hopeless, it just means that you could use some help.

B = The Pushback Procrastinator:

Research indicates that the Pushback Procrastinator is the profile with the biggest population, close to forty percent of Procrastination Profile Quiz-takers. You're certainly not alone! While you'd like to change, your pattern is to resist it. That doesn't mean you're a bad person, you just find yourself pushing back against anything that feels like "should", "must", or "ought to". Unfortunately, that has unhappy consequences. You want people to accept you for who you are, whether you follow through or not. By resisting and ducking you not only abdicate your responsibility, but you also give up your dreams. You *don't* need a brain transplant in order to change this, though – really! If you're ready, it's time to enlist the help of friends and family to remind you whenever you slip into resistance mode, and be open to assistance that will aid you in seeing your pattern in a new light.

C = The Almost Anticrastinator:

You're almost there! All you need is more realistic scheduling, and some measures in place to ensure that things don't slip through the cracks. You've already made a good effort toward procrastination elimination, and your system needs some tweaking. Make sure *all* your goals are worthwhile pursuing, and start a system of rewards and consequences that makes sense for your personality. If you've tried this, and are still not making headway, consider that perfectionism may be stopping you. If you feel like you're already "dancing as fast as you can", and you still "aren't there", it's time to take a closer look at what may be going on, and for that you may want an outside, objective perspective, or at least a few radical strategies.

D = The Awakening Procrastinator:

You've only begun to recognize that there are systems available and steps you can take to prevent procrastination from costing you dearly. While you may feel uncomfortable using calendars and to-do lists, they're honestly not as much work as you might think. Take a closer look at what you're not doing, and focus on one thing at a time. Plan the steps to complete that task and use your calendar to schedule the actions required. If available, start using a computer date book with a reminder system which always runs in the background, or send yourself voicemail reminders to trigger follow through action. These work well because they don't rely on you alone to remember. Better yet, because these are new skills, it will really help to get some outside assistance, such as books or websites that address procrastination. Even better, a coach can help you tailor your approach so you're much less likely to get frustrated and give up.

E = The Overwhelmed Procrastinator:

Help! While we all get overwhelmed occasionally, you experience this most of the time, sometimes even giving up. Although others originally gave you a "procrastinator" identity, you've come to believe this label really applies. But it's only a habit you've come to rely on based on that label. Many people have successfully thrown off that identity and have begun to embrace their inner anticrastinator. You've definitely done many things on time, so focus your attention there. Start by choosing small goals, applying what you have used in past successes. Build on your already ample experience of successfully following through in many areas. Take advantage of offers of help, but don't look for a knight on a white horse to finish your tasks or projects for you. Sign up for programs and courses to help you to accomplish your goals in a timely way. Seek outside assistance to help you get on track; that's what it's there for!

F = The Fabulous-At-Following-Through Anticrastinator:

Congratulations on slaying those delayer demons. You've learned how to be optimally productive and effective, and it's likely you're experiencing success in most, if not all, areas of your life. If you're already really good at following through but want to be even better, good for you. There are plenty of strategies to help you kick up your productivity and effectiveness a few notches.

It may be that you're taking this quiz because someone in your life is a procrastinator, and it affects you. If so, be aware that nagging and judging that person is completely counterproductive, no matter what their profile. Knowing their profile is helpful to understanding them and working with them. If what you've tried hasn't worked, please contact me if you're interested in making a successful change in this area.

Scoring for questions 6-11:

For each **a** answer you chose, give yourself 5 points

For each **b** answer you chose, give yourself 3 points

For each **c** answer you chose, give yourself 1 point

20–30 points: Hey, congratulate yourself! You're probably not procrastinating as badly as you might have thought. You've developed the skills to take action, just not quite as rigorously as you'd like. You're not a superhero, and there will always be room for improvement. Focus on your successes, and use those successes to conquer other areas of procrastination. Enlarge your support networks, keep your eye on the goal, and be wary of the lure of perfectionism. To improve toward optimal use of your time and energy, enroll in a program targeted toward your goal, buddy with others, and find other ways to place yourself in an environment that will pull you to the success you want.

10–20 points: Lots of people are in the same boat, and while that's no excuse, at least it may feel less of a burden. You've recognized that the dues you've been paying as a member of the Procrastinator's Club are too high, and it's time to end your membership. Observe and reach out to people who are accomplishing more. Find out what they're doing and start experimenting with new habits and new attitudes. Invest in the time and effort of being coached whether informally by friends or by a trained professional. Always look for what you can do, rather than what you're not doing.

6–10 points: If there's one thing you shouldn't put off, it's seeking assistance right away to avert tragedy, disaster, or at the very least, misery. Seek counseling, and keep in mind that this is an opportunity for you to grow, learn, and create a new beginning. You need some help in creating a sense of possibility and support in helping you make small decisions that give you more and more confidence to turn over a new leaf. There are no-cost and low-cost options, including reading books from the library, watching or listening to self-improvement television and radio shows, and counseling programs through your town, county, state, or province, or through non-profit organizations.

Strategy 1:

Embrace Your Imperfections ...and Stop Trying to be Normal!

Strategy 1:

Embrace Your Imperfections ... And Stop Trying to be Normal!

The Pressure of Perfection Provokes Procrastination

We all know we're not perfect, and that we never will be, but that doesn't stop many of us from trying. Intellectually, we consider the idea of being flawless as ridiculous. At the same time, there is a lot of cultural emphasis on being Number One. As a society, we have little respect or admiration for Number Two. There's more pressure than ever to be buff, beautiful, smart, sexy, successful, wealthy, and wise, and to be as close to "the best" as possible, because less than the best just doesn't count.

While most of us are still attempting to reach our own personal version of ideal, or at least as close as we can get to it, we still get tied up in how we're far less than perfect. The standard is now so hard to reach that some people have given up hope completely and let themselves go to pot. A lot of us would be happy just to feel normal.

How many times each day does your concern about not being right enough, smart enough, rich enough, or thin enough affect how you interact with people, or influence your decisions? I'm guessing that if you paid close attention, there would be dozens, from how you dress and eat, to the way you speak to people, the kinds of tasks you're willing to take on, and the company you keep.

At Least Acceptable?

Here's an experiment: look at what you're wearing and think back to this morning and how you decided to wear those clothes. How did you feel about yourself when you chose them? What made you decide on them rather than some other choice? Think about the general style of clothes you wear and how you came to choose that style. Are you a conservative dresser or more of a non-conformist? Are most of your clothes formal, business attire, or casual? Are your clothes fairly loose or are they more fitted? What were the personal beliefs behind your choices? How much did fitting in or looking acceptable influence your choices?

Not that fitting in is a bad thing, it's just overrated. We're social animals, after all, and for millennia fitting in was crucial for our survival. I'm simply drawing your attention to how this normal human desire, beyond its basic function, operates in your own life and could backfire when given too much significance.

What happens when you lose the clothes game (trying on different outfits, none of which seem to complement you and finally giving up in frustration), or when you have a "bad hair day"? How does it affect your energy level and motivation?

You probably wonder what this has to do with overcoming procrastination, right? Well, read on.

Perfection Paralysis

Have you noticed that whenever you find yourself lacking in some way your productivity level plummets? Have you noticed that when you or others make disparaging remarks about your abilities, it negatively influences your effectiveness? Have you ever been almost paralyzed with a sense of not being good enough, and been stuck there for a few hours, weeks, or even years?

When some of our efforts meet with failure, we begin to doubt our own capabilities. Everyone has different levels of self-confidence, depending on levels of innate confidence and drive, parental influence, and life experience. Based on past social training in being "realistic," many of us have constructed a thick and sticky layer of self-doubt. The mistakes we make, the feedback and "advice" we get from others, and the difficulties we come across create a swamp of uneasiness about our worth. This results in a fear that we won't be successful, so we stop trying, or at least trying as hard. "It's too risky, too hard," we tell ourselves, "Why bother?" Psychologists call this "learned helplessness" and it's a huge factor in procrastination, particularly amongst more severe procrastinators. Some people internalize their guilt, holding themselves responsible. Other people externalize it, blaming others or their circumstances.

If you're someone who beats yourself up for putting things off, you may be relieved to know that it may be easier for you to change than someone who places responsibility elsewhere. We all define ourselves by our past experiences. It may be a long time since you've had successes. You may be more open to improvement and attaining your dreams. Why? Because you're already equipped to accept your contribution to your procrastination situation and you're ready to find your way out.

What is Normal?

In 2005 the American Psychiatric Association stated that one fifth of Americans suffer from a diagnosable mental disorder during any given year. Other reputable organizations put the number at one third. If in any given year that many of us are a least a little crazy in the head, then what is "normal"?

We spend so much energy, time, money, and heartache trying to fit in with what we believe is acceptable, when we'd be happier and better off applying our resources to recognizing and embracing our own quirky gifts, talents, interests, and idiosyncrasies. Sure, we're willing to tolerate the less-than-fabulous qualities in celebrities and other famous people. We're able to take the wheat with the chaff when there's something notable, popular, or noble about them. But we're not so generous with ourselves, our family members, friends, co-workers or someone we meet at a barbeque.

Let's face it. A lot of us are pretty unforgiving about ourselves and others.

Some of this pressure helps prompt us into action toward better habits, so it can be helpful. All too commonly, though, there comes a point of diminishing returns, and rather than acting as a stimulus, the pressure becomes an excuse to lock ourselves into an uncomfortable prison of self-loathing. Oh, we don't hate everything about ourselves, but beneath a veneer of mature capability and confidence there's a frightened kid terrified of being exposed as not-good-enough. Those who fit Procrastinator Profiles A, D, and E have lots of practice in this. (See the Procrastinator Profiler Quiz.)

Every Profile has its Benefits, and its Challenges

As a culture, we've identified procrastination as a character defect that fits squarely into the profile of a loser. In my professional capacity (as well as in my personal life) almost everyone I meet – even if they're accomplished, financially successful, and enjoy a rich social life – believes they procrastinate and are ashamed of it.

Most people procrastinate somewhere in their personal or professional lives. There are some people who were born with, or have developed an intolerance for, letting things wait. While you might be jealous of them, or derisively call them anal retentive – or maybe both! – they're not a whole lot different from you. They're as uncomfortable having things hang over their head as you are uncomfortable facing the challenging task of getting on with them. You get your relief by not dealing with the situation; they get their relief by putting their obligations behind them

Believe it or not, there is a downside to being an *anticrastinator.* When you're impatient to get things done, you tend to hurry. You miss details, make compromises in quality, or hastily make decisions in an attempt to finish quickly. You might end up completing work that you later find was unnecessary.

Neither letting everything slide indefinitely nor doing everything immediately are effective as stand-alone game plans. Instead, tasks and situations need to be evaluated individually, and your plan then based on those variables. Condemning yourself for being imperfect, and condemning others for doing things differently from you are both unconstructive...and they don't make you any friends, either!

Excuses, Excuses!

If you're inclined to make excuses for why you don't get things done, and tend to abdicate your accountability, it could be that you're denying your own limitations (Procrastinator Profiler B). You've created stories to excuse yourself, and you've derived some comfort from that. In the end, though, is that what you want to continue to choose?

Yes, there are factors that are part of why you've done (or should we say not done) certain things. That hasn't stopped many very successful people who have had huge external forces working against them. They didn't allow those forces to thwart them.

If you're anything like everyone else I know, your parents, teachers, friends, bosses, spouses, and children often ask with exasperation, "What is **wrong** with you?" when you do something they don't like, value, or agree with.

I know I heard that many, many times when growing up, and it wasn't long before I came to believe that there was something wrong with me. Indeed, I heard it so often that I couldn't help but think there was very little **right** about me. Since I couldn't let anyone else see that in case they rejected me,

I spent a lot of time and effort hiding what was wrong. Aside from a lot of fear, self-loathing, regretted decisions, bad relationships, and dysfunctional behaviors, it led to loads of procrastination.

When I came to realize this in early adulthood, I made another common mistake: blaming my parents. I spent a lot of energy and gave up a lot of time and potential by putting the fault for my weaknesses on my mom and dad. It was years before I recognized that I wasn't any happier doing that, nor was that pattern – making them responsible for how I was so far from perfect – helping me to improve myself in any way.

What's amazing is that very few people have been lucky enough to avoid this scenario, so I've got lots of company! No, I'm not perfect. In fact, darn far from it. But nobody else is perfect either, and that levels the playing field. The truth is, we're all acceptable, despite our shortcomings. Most of our difficulties have been caused through **self-doubt** about our abilities or worth, rather than because we really lacked that ability or worth.

Expectations can be Harmful to Your Productivity!

Doris, a writer and radio show host, was unhappy with herself because she rarely had dinner on the table at 6 pm, she always let the laundry pile up until she needed a hazmat suit to step into the laundry room. In addition, her home-office desk looked like someone had fought a paper war on it. The truth was, she hated domestic tasks, but her mom had set such a good example for her that Doris felt like a sham as a mom. Not only was she not perfect, she thought, but she wasn't even normal. Through discussing the situation, Doris realized that her family was neither undernourished nor lacking in clean clothes, and that her expectations weren't reasonable. Unlike Doris, her mom didn't work full-time outside the house, and life is far more complex and faster-paced now than it had been forty years ago. Since Doris loathed housework (which is something she shares with many women) she was thrilled to realize that she could readily, and without regret, junk the drive to be super-mom.

She, her husband, and her kids often had activities that prevented them from eating together at 6 pm. Her happy alternative would be to keep healthy foods in the house, and order out when appropriate, lessening her burden. Even though the laundry piled up, it did eventually get done. She could find whatever she needed on her desk, and since it was the family's catch-all location for papers, she decided to designate a different catch-all spot for them, so her desk was limited to her own paperwork.

Through embracing your shortcomings, instead of punishing yourself for having them, your entire attitude lightens. The burden of your perceived failings will fall away like a stone, freeing your energy and enthusiasm.

Being Satisfied Versus Being Number One

If you're willing to look with open eyes, you'll notice that everyone you meet has some gift, noble trait, endearing quality, wise perspective, surprising skill, or other hidden or more obvious, gem.

I'm not talking about the old "everyone is unique and therefore special" cliché. Ugh. Gag me. I'm asking you to play with the possibility that just because someone doesn't do things your way, they're not necessarily wrong, and may actually be bringing something really valuable to the table. To paraphrase a truly corny chain email I recently got, just because you're smarter or richer or more fashionable doesn't mean you're better than someone else, it only means you're blessed in those areas. And there, but for the grace of God, go you.

The truth is, you'll probably never be Number One, and even if you do get there, you won't be there for long. Wanting to be Number One isn't bad in and of itself. There's a difference, though between a want and a need. What happens to a lot of people is that they turn a want into a need to be Number One, then they become miserable that they aren't. Want is a desire, something that you work toward and make progress with, hopefully enjoying the journey. Need is heavily laden with expectation, pressure, and judgment.

Similarly, just because you're not as "cool" as someone you admire doesn't mean you don't have a lot going for you. Because our brains are so attuned to criticism, it's easy to see the negative, and this blinds us to many of our shining characteristics.

Better Versus Perfect

Now, you won't be able to just snap your fingers and be forever improved. You're going to have to remind yourself (or have others remind you) of that whenever you find yourself wallowing in Loser Land.

Linda is married and has three kids. She's a stay-at-home mom. She had attended a presentation I had given on getting organized because she was tired of the clutter and chaos in her household and hadn't found a way to handle it herself. She hired me because even though her mother had been tidy, she hadn't learned those habits for herself, and didn't feel good about it. She loved her wife and mother roles, and wanted to be better at them. To the world, she presented herself as a pretty "together" person. She dressed nicely, was well-groomed and well-spoken. But behind that was an uncomfortable sense that she wasn't "normal" because she wasn't a naturally neat person, and because she regularly put things off.

Some people are born with a more linear or left-brain orientation. These people approach problems using logic, sequence, and analysis. They're "splitters," breaking things down into categories. They often find it easy to be organized.

Other people are more intuitive or right-brained, and use feelings, see connections, resemblances, and think holistically. They are "lumpers," and have a tendency to synthesize and look at wholes. For this group, being organized often requires a new way of thinking, and the development of a new set of skills. Through our discussions, Linda discovered that she was right-brained. She also had never really had the motivation or incentive to learn to be more organized until recently. When she was young, her mom did all the cooking, cleaning, and laundry for Linda and her sister. Linda married early, and had the help of a nanny in raising her kids. The nanny did much of the household work, and her husband made many of the decisions.

For the last few years, Linda wanted to grow beyond what she knew, but she kept berating herself for not being "better", and hadn't made much progress. As we worked together, and I continually assured her that she was already capable and wonderful, she became more open to acquiring new habits and using new tools. She was able to tolerate her own "mistakes" and forgive herself for not being completely and immediately successful in her progress, rather than allowing her "failures" to throw her off track. This flexibility didn't mean that she let herself off the hook completely, but instead gave her added motivation to find better methods, and to keep trying.

Replacing a longstanding habit or belief takes time. It won't die a quick death. You've got an investment in maintaining your habits, as uncomfortable as that sounds. Ironically, that discomfort is still in your comfort zone. Change is just beyond the threshold. Maybe you, like I did, fear that letting go of self-reproach is a slippery slope that might unleash a fiercer monster, one who is more irresponsible, uncaring, unproductive, and unmotivated. It's understandable that you'd be afraid of that, but do you really, honestly think that you'd allow that to happen? My experience with hundreds of clients and workshop participants leads me to seriously doubt it.

You may be uncertain about what to expect of yourself once you start being more self-compassionate. This uncertainty can feel more distressing than your familiar sense of unease. Don't worry, that's a very normal part of the process of change. You've invested time and money to read this far, and you've done so because you trust that there is information here that can help you; that I've helped many other people using the same techniques. Why not try this idea on for size, and see what happens? Give it a couple of weeks and play with forgiving yourself, even if you think you really are at fault. Instead of disparaging yourself, see what you need to do now to correct the situation, and what you can do in the future to prevent it from happening again. You can always run back into your little hole of self-criticism if you really want to.

Putting Strategy Number One to Work

What responsibilities (such as parent, spouse, business owner, employee, homeowner, volunteer) do you have?

_____

_____

If everyone else you knew of was in your situation, or if your situation was more socially acceptable (for example, if being voluptuous and not very fit was in fashion, or if having clutter was considered a sign of prosperity, or if putting off your project allowed you do to more important things) would you still want to pursue this goal?

Yes _____

No _____

Where among your responsibilities are you ready to start embracing your imperfections?

_____

_____

Look at your list of to-do items. If you don't have a list, make one. Which items have you been procrastinating about because it feels daunting to meet some high expectation?

_____

_____

_____

Pick one item. What are the expectations?

_____

_____

What's the worst that could happen if you did only a passable job, rather than a completely fabulous one?

_____

_____

Realistically, how likely is it that the worst will happen?

_____

_____

What is the next step you know you have to take to handle this particular item?

_____

_____

What day, at what time, can you schedule twenty to sixty minutes into your calendar today, tomorrow, or this or next week to start?

_____

_____

What can you tell yourself that feels more flexible than the self-critical thoughts you usually have? What would be a more validating phrase that could motivate rather than drain you?

_____

_____

Strategy 2:

Drop Your Tired Old Goals – at Least for the Moment

Strategy 2:

Drop Your Tired Old Goals Completely

N o, I'm not crazy. You know those desires you keep beating yourself up about? The ones you've never been able to accomplish or maintain? I want you to drop those goals, at least for the moment. Maybe forever.

It seems pretty counter-intuitive, doesn't it?

Common Goals

Have you been trying to lose weight or get in shape for years or, like Linda in the previous chapter, trying to finally get yourself organized? Maybe you've wanted to get a handle on your financial situation, or there's a book or other writing project you've wanted to start (or finish)? My procrastination survey of hundreds of people showed that these are the top goals for which people haven't yet found a sustainable solution.

You've probably made a number of attempts at following through on these goals, and it's likely you've had some small successes here and there over the long course of battle with this demon goal. Good for you! It's not as though you've forever been completely and utterly ignoring the situation, is it?

If you've taken the Procrastinator Profiler Quiz, and you're an E profile, it may be that you've given up and are feeling guilty and ashamed. Or perhaps you make little mincing attempts without any consistency; then you're probably an A or a D profile. There are those of us who start off strong and then taper off; something inspires us temporarily, but we lose sight of it (or, more appropriately, connection with it) over the longer haul.

These kinds of "historical" goals aren't typical accomplishments, but rather the result of months or years of continually applying effort and resolve. You must decide daily (with some of them, many times each day), or weekly to persist toward your objective. These aren't fast and finished decisions and deeds that are quickly done and out of the way, but require much, much more of us. To be successful with our goals may require lifetime commitment. After all, if we lose weight, we need to keep it off. Once we get organized, we have to put effort into staying that way. Once we create a financial plan, we have to follow it over decades to achieve the financial independence and stability we want.

Give some thought, right now, to what it would take to bring long term success with your long-time unachieved aspirations. What do you think it would really require from you?

Sometimes we don't pursue goals because we haven't created the psychic space to be inspired or motivated Or we haven't found a system that works for us, or we don't understand what we need to know to make a positive change. That's a quick fix, and not the kind of goal I'm referring to with this strategy.

No, I'm talking about those goals for which we're all looking (and hoping and praying) for a magic bullet, something that guarantees our success over the long run, with little effort or sacrifice on our part. There are an awful lot of people making boatloads of money offering magic bullets to achieve permanent victory over these gremlins. They work partially, or for a little while, but unless we make a significant shift in belief or perspective, we soon go back to our old ways.

What's required to make a lasting transformation to any of those kinds of goals? You need an internal shift of deep significance. It's likely that in some area of your life, you've already experienced some profound internal shift. This is pretty rare, and usually generated by either an abrupt and surprising (usually shocking) event or a long slow slide to the bottom, and often – but not always – involves considerable pain. You may be really lucky and connect with someone or something that inspires you with truly lasting effect. It does sometimes happen, but it's unusual, and you can't depend on when or if it will happen.

Be Discriminating

This is why you have to be discriminating about the initiatives you're willing to put your time and effort into – pick your battles, so to speak. You've spent large amounts of time and effort (and money) living with the situation or trying to change things, with little result. You suffered lots of frustration and unhappiness when you didn't succeed.

Consider what life would be like if you put aside some or all of the historical goals that, for you, have been the biggest bugaboos, the ones that you've been wrestling with for years.

Provided these goals are not a real and immediate threat to your life, I'm giving you permission, for the next seventy-two hours, to experiment with dropping all of them.

Oooh, pretty scary, isn't it, and at the same time, a huge relief? Or perhaps you think I'm an idiot for suggesting it, or that it's an absurd idea. Good! That's expected and normal. This isn't called a *radical* strategy for nothing!

I've found that playing with letting these goals go has fascinating and productive results. It's like dumping ballast out of a ship or a hot air balloon. As the dead weight is released, the ship skips more swiftly across the waves, the balloon immediately rises, with no extra energy needed to power the movement.

It's Just an Experiment

Understand that I'm not suggesting that you must give up your old goals, nor that you will never be successful at achieving them. I'm not even suggesting that using traditional methods won't work. Those kinds of approaches do work, but they take effort, struggle, and friction, and they suffer from a lack of sustainability. No matter what your procrastination profile is, you've experienced how exhausting dependence on sheer will power is, and how short-lived its effect too.

Dumping your old goals makes way for a completely different outlook, and opens up avenues and approaches that were previously invisible. In order for this to work properly, you have to experiment with dropping the goal entirely, not just try to think up a new approach. Give yourself the chance to release it and see what that feels like. You'll come face to face with one of two things:

1. You become aware of how stifling this goal has been for you, and how much

better you feel without that weight on your shoulders. It's now apparent that although this goal may seem "good for you", you're really not motivated enough to pursue it, compared with other objectives you're working toward. While you could be richer, healthier, or thinner, the truth is that the amount of effort, work, and time really just isn't worth it to you. You can give up feeling bad about yourself and happy that you've made a decision not to spend any more time and energy on it.

2. The thought of dropping your "historical" goal is horrifying to you. If this is your reaction, great! It gives you the opportunity to explore what is really important to you about the goal. What would it mean to you or about you if you achieved it? What might it mean to you or about you if you never achieved it? Are you willing to play with ditching the goal long enough to find out? There may be some pivotal information that will be revealed through taking a closer look.

That information can make the difference between wallowing in continued delay versus making clear decisions on which you can take immediate action.

If you're a Procrastination Profile B, you may have a tendency to hang on to how "life" or other people (like your spouse, kids, boss, or parents) are to blame for your inability to achieve your goal.

While it may (or may not!) be true that your circumstances make it more challenging to follow through on your goal, recognize that you've been making a choice to use those circumstances to absolve you of your responsibility for reaching the goal.

If that's the case, you might resist letting go of your old goals. You'll really be on your own now, and it's understandable that your resistance is likely to increase before you're willing to change. That's not a character flaw, so don't bother judging yourself. It won't help you stop procrastinating in any case!

The results of the Procrastinator Profiler show that B profiles are three times more common than A, B, D, or F, and more than twice as common as C, so you've got lots of company.

Is the old goal too rigid and unforgiving? That brings up an almost immediate internal battle. If that's what you're facing, drop the old goal entirely, or at least significantly enough to change the outcome.

Quitting on Quitting?

Karla had wanted to give up smoking for quite a few years. She'd been able to quit for a few days here and there, and had even once quit for over a year, but she'd gone back to it. By the time we started working on this habit, she felt somewhat hopeless about permanently quitting. Every Sunday she'd tell herself that she'd quit on Monday, but she'd find herself with another cigarette by the next weekend, if not earlier. Of course, she knew that smoking was bad for her and that she needed to quit, but there wasn't enough incentive to make it worth giving up forever.

It turned out that what really bothered her was never, ever being able to smoke another cigarette again for the rest of her life. You can see how the goal of quitting forever brought up immediate inner conflict. It was no wonder she was having so much trouble with that goal!

I asked her if she could drop the idea of quitting forever, because it was a goal that wasn't currently palatable or sustainable for her.

What if she could allow herself one cigarette per month? She'd be greatly reducing the health impact of a half-to-full-pack a day habit, but wouldn't be locking herself into never, ever smoking again. The commitment to a maximum of one cigarette per month closed the door to any more than that, yet was flexible enough that it provided an incentive for good behavior. It may seem backwards to you to reward quitting with having a cigarette, but it worked to greatly reduce Karla's dependence on her habit and the resulting impact on her health (and family and finances). In the four years since making this decision, Karla has found that there are times when she goes three or four months between cigarettes. A couple of times she failed to limit her cigarette smoking to one per month and had two, but the flexibility of the commitment was workable enough to prevent her from going back to anything more than that.

Grieving Over Goals

Sometimes the goals we have to give up are close to our hearts – as opposed to something that's "in our best interests" like Karla's situation above. It's counter-intuitive to even consider abandoning our more heartfelt desires, and we feel a lot of resistance to even the idea. At the core of that resistance is sadness and grief for what we believe could have been.

For years, Jo had wanted her own thriving change management business, making a difference in the world. She'd been trying to establish it successfully but was struggling to make it financially sustainable. As an interim measure, she'd applied for a human resources consulting contract with a humanitarian organization, applying the skills and experiences she'd used in previous jobs. She'd won the contract, but felt that focusing on it instead of her change management business meant that she was giving up the dream she'd been pushing and striving for. She didn't want to let it go, but she needed the income that the contract provided. I asked her to play with shelving (for now) the business goals she'd been pursuing and focus strictly on the contract work.

Jo had to allow herself to hang with the discomfort of leaving those goals behind. She discovered sorrow; this was part of a pattern in her life of having to move on while leaving things behind. It took a week or two before she could give herself permission to feel okay about it. Once she did, she quickly found that she had a new challenge: to position herself for a contract extension. Within three months, she was so successful at her work that the client asked to use her change management skills. Instead of being a diversion from her business, this new contract was now a direct and substantial revenue stream for that business. This was something she never expected – and couldn't foresee – but letting go of her long-held goal was what made it possible.

By ditching the goals she'd been clinging to, she was quicker in achieving them. How fabulously ironic is that??

Putting Strategy Number Two to Work

List your historical goals and how long you've been pursuing each of them:

Goal   How long

_____ _____

_____ _____

_____ _____

_____ _____

_____ _____

Which of these goals are you willing to experiment with dropping first?

_____

_____

What do you think would happen if you let this goal go?

_____

_____

What occurs to you when you think about really dropping it? How do you feel about it? What feels good? Is there anything that doesn't feel so good?

_____

_____

What other heartfelt goals or projects might you feel free to pursue if you were at least temporarily released from this goal and any guilt for having dropped it?

_____

_____

For how long would you like to experiment with dropping this goal?

_____

_____

Strategy 3:

Hire a Hit Man
to Kill You
if You Don't Follow Through

Strategy 3:

Hire a Hit Man to Kill You if You Don't Follow Through

O kay, so I don't mean this literally. But you get the drift, don't you? You want to make putting it off harder than following through.

Want to Versus Have To

Research into procrastination (published in the *Journal of Social Behavior and Personality* in 2000) indicates that "want to" projects – those that are self-initiated for the purposes of enjoyment or improvement – are much more likely to be put off than "have to" projects, those that are more externally motivated to meet some obligation. In fact, in one study, where the summer projects of adults were examined, more than three times as many "want to" projects were never started as compared to "have to" projects. Twice as many "have to" projects were successfully completed compared to "want to" projects.

So here's the lesson: stop waiting for inspiration. Stop waiting until you're "ready".

Many of my clients have the idea that they can't be creative unless they're inspired, and that inspiration can't be scheduled. So they find other things to do, and they wait, in vain. Their goals sit high on a shelf, waiting for the ever-expected visit by their muse, and gather dust by the day. Other goals get piled on top, and before you know it, you can't even find your beloved dream. It's buried under a mountain of other "want to" projects.

As the days, weeks, and months go by, your internal shame-o-meter registers higher and higher readings. What I'm asking you to do is make the stakes high enough to get that shame-o-meter to redline.

It's possible to make a "have to" out of a "want to". In other words, by assigning a negative consequence to not following through, the task you want to work on will then feel more like a requirement and less like something easily shrugged off. You're creating a probability rather than just a possibility.

Here's where a little imagination goes a long way. You've probably tried versions of this in the past. Some of them may have worked, and some have failed.

If you're avoiding a "have to" task, you just haven't made the "have to" powerful enough to motivate you.

WARNING: If the "have to" obligations you're ignoring or not handling could result in your losing your job, your marriage, or your home (or something else very important to you) seek help immediately. **Don't take the time to attempt to change on your own.** You've probably tried this with limited results. There is no time to waste. Contact a qualified professional because you need outside assistance. Put this book down right now, call or email a counselor, therapist, or coach, and make an appointment to get started right away. Ask your friends or relatives to help you to see it through.

Using the Past to Assist the Future

Thankfully, most of us aren't in that situation. If your procrastination isn't severe, be grateful! From a coping perspective, those more burdened with this habit are not bad people, they just have lower expectations relating to their success, so they generally apply less effort. There's a wide spectrum from severely dysfunctional to optimally functional, with a wide range in between.

Where are you on the spectrum right now? Where you find yourself may fluctuate with various goals and at different times in your life, depending on recent successes or less-than-successes, personal or professional circumstances, or even the state of the economy.

Of course, blaming your dawdling on exterior circumstances, while making you temporarily feel better, isn't going to help you get what you really want. Unless, of course, what would really make you fulfilled, content, and satisfied is to live a pale, second-rate version of what's possible for you, and you enjoy relying on excuses to justify it. Is that you? I don't think so; you wouldn't be reading this if that were the case.

Instead, recall some of your previous successes with getting things done on time. What can you identify as the factors that spurred you to complete them by their deadline?

Hiring the Right Hit Man for You

The other day, one of my clients tried to get out of her appointment. Terry dearly wants to write a book, and she's a superb writer. Her writing is hip, witty, funny, and incisive, and enjoyable to read. But writing the book terrifies her. In addition to writing, she's doing contract work for an organization, and was allowing that work to fill all her time beyond necessary or reasonable limits, and to take complete priority over her own project. By setting no boundary around the contract work, she was able to avoid a good deal of the discomfort of writing her own book, having an excuse to put the project off.

But knowing that she hired me to help her follow through, I wouldn't let her wiggle out of our appointment. Through our conversation, I prompted her to create a goal for the next time we talked, and followed that with scheduling times on her calendar. Previous experience taught me that she might ignore those self-made appointments.

Recently, we'd agreed that if she didn't get the product of her writing goal emailed to me by a certain hour that she'd have to pay me an extra $50. She'd followed through, but admitted she'd thought to herself more than once, "To hell with it, I'll just pay her the damn $50 and be done with it." But she didn't want to disappoint me. She confessed that money wasn't the incentive (at least, that amount of money), but humiliation was something she didn't want to experience. We identified humiliation as her "hit man," and designed the next step toward achieving her goal with that in mind: she scheduled an hour of writing for the next day and would email me at the end of the hour as to whether she followed through or not.

Lo and behold, the next day, a few minutes after the end of the hour, an email arrived from Terry. She'd written two paragraphs, and while her email was mostly just to say she had written something, she felt inspired and was planning to write more in the evening. The best part was that she'd followed through instead of disregarding her writing appointment. It was a victory, and it felt delicious. Terry had identified and hired a hit man to make sure she followed through. She'd invested in hiring a coach and made twice-weekly appointments. Added to that, she had been honest and open in crafting a way to make it easier for her to follow through than not to: humiliation is a potent hit man! It was enough of a pinch for Terry to make the time and effort to persist in making progress on her objective.

A Little Procrastination Math

You see, any time we procrastinate, there are always warring desires, commitments, or beliefs that are responsible. If there weren't any conflict, we'd make a decision to do something and it would get done without a problem. Take a look at anything you've been putting off, and you'll see this at work.

Here's a set of equations that may help explain this:

Your goal minus warring desire = result

Here's how it applies to common procrastination situations:

Wanting to losing weight minus being hungry and loving to eat = one pound gained.

Getting receipts together for taxes minus tedium and more interesting things to do = requesting a tax filing extension.

Desire for a serenely and efficiently organized space minus not wanting to throw away "perfectly good" stuff and feeling overwhelmed by how long you think it will take = growing piles of papers + stuffed files, closets, basements, attics

Terry wants to write a book, but also has warring beliefs in the form of doubts about whether she has anything valuable to say, whether she'll be able to finish, whether anyone will actually buy the book, and so on. She also has competing commitments, such as a young family to attend to and contract work she needs to complete that pays her immediate money. But she really wants to increase the odds for success in completing her book.

How much do you want to achieve your goal? What, and how powerful, are the warring desires, commitments, or beliefs associated with it? These factors directly determine how easy or hard it is for you to follow through.

Okay, so now the question is: how do you balance this equation a little more toward the "getting it done" side? Hiring a hit man adds weight and heft to the goal side of the equation.

If you want to lose weight, you might add a buddy to help hold your feet to the fire, sign up for an event that requires you to wear a swimsuit, or hire a personal trainer or nutritionist to help create and maintain a program.

Usually, a financial or social investment is more compelling emotionally. If you go off your plan, you could add a consequence of, say, giving a sizable donation to the charity you hate the most, doing a favor for someone you really can't stand, or something else that (for you) will be distasteful enough to persuade you to follow through with your goal. It needs to fit you, and to be only slightly more painful than what it takes to get the job done.

Pick a Whack That Will Hurt

If you do this and still don't follow through, you simply haven't hired a strong enough hit man. Go back to the drawing board. What have you identified that has motivated you in the past? What would you hate doing even more than what you've been putting off? Whose help can you call on to make sure you don't blow it off?

Who (or what) is your hit man? You may have a variety of them. Everyone is different, and what works for someone else may not work for you. Willingness to be frank and truthful with yourself will reveal it. The hit man has to hurt at least a little, or it won't be effective and will backfire.

A few years ago, I read a success story about a man who was overweight and wanted to go on a diet. He hated to cook, and he usually ate in restaurants. He knew he'd be likely to lose weight if he wasn't able to eat out, so he came up with a novel solution. He made up "Wanted" posters featuring his picture, and offered anyone who saw him in a restaurant a $1000 reward. He posted these in all the restaurants he usually ate in, and in other places where he often went. This was a powerful hit man for him, enough so that he accomplished his goal and his story landed in the news.

Once you find a successful hit man, it may work for you forever, but it might start losing its punch after a while. That's normal. Be creative and get help in devising a new one.

Putting Strategy Number Three to Work

Write down one significant goal that you've putting off, one that you really want to stop putting off:

_____

_____

What is the next step you know you need to take to achieve this goal?

_____

_____

What methods have you already tried that haven't worked?

_____

_____

_____

What was it about those methods that didn't work for you?

_____

_____

_____

What methods have you tried with other goals that worked for you?

_____

_____

_____

What was it about those methods that motivated you?

_____

_____

_____

How might you adjust your successful methods for this particular application?

_____

_____

_____

What day and time are you committing to taking the next step with this goal? You needn't work on it for any more than a half hour on this date and time:

Date:_____   Time: _____

What are the consequences you will assign, the "hitman you will hire" for not following through? Remember, they have to pinch!

_____

_____

_____

Who could you call on for help with this goal or accountability with the hitman?

_____

_____

_____

Strategy 4:

Don't Take Yes
For an Answer

Strategy 4:

Don't Take Yes For an Answer

Most of the time when we add something to our to-do list, we don't really give much thought to whether it's something that we really need to do or not, how we might accomplish it, or whether we're really committed to doing so. This strategy is a twist on an old cliché. Don't take yes for an answer. I mean your own unexamined, unplanned yes.

Before you include anything on your to-do list, it needs a brief examination. Could it be you're just telling yourself you'll do something without real intent and strategy to follow through? Don't bother. You know what happens: you say you'll do it, and then you ignore it, deny it, forget it, put it off, say you'll do it just after you finish reading the paper, or your email, or when the television show is over, or just after you call your friend. You believe you have good intentions. And for the most part, you do, especially when you create the intention!

Are Your Intentions Serious?

Stop just intending. Intention without action is like a car without wheels; you may have a vehicle, but it's really hard to get anywhere.

When you catch yourself making a promise to take care of something, recognize that your tendency is to postpone it until another time. Don't bother making that promise. Why? It's a recipe for failure and another blow to your internal Capability Barometer. When you don't follow through, you lose faith in your general ability to achieve your goals and intentions. Later, in future tasks, lowered confidence means you expend less effort because you expect less success. It becomes a vicious cycle.

Jessica had a lot of newspapers and magazines, amongst other stuff she wanted to get rid of. We talked about what she'd gain from getting rid of all her clutter and finally getting her apartment organized, and she seemed enthusiastic. While Jessica seemed to really want to change things, she wasn't serious about her intentions. While the thought of an organized home was quite alluring, being surrounded with piles of papers, bags, and boxes was more comfortable for her. I recommended that Jessica speak with a psychiatrist about it, but she never made the calls, even though she promised to a number of times. It became apparent that de-cluttering wasn't important enough for her, and there wasn't enough of a cost for having it that she was motivated to take action. In the end, Jessica realized that ridding herself of her clutter wasn't a task that she was currently serious enough about to work on, and we focused on other initiatives instead.

The Influence of Belief over Intention

If I believed that by giving up sweets forever I could look like Nicole Kidman, would I do it? You bet! But I don't believe that just by giving up sweets I could achieve that wish, so I don't bother putting myself to the test. (I'm a normal size but, like most women these days, I'd like to be a few pounds lighter.)

If you believed that by making a list of five significant but reasonable daily tasks and following through with them could make you a millionaire, would you do it? Probably, but do you believe it? Most likely not. Yet there are a number of people who are now millionaires because they believed just such a thing and they acted on it.

When Carlos called me the first time, he felt somewhat hopeless. A successful businessman, he believed that his 24/7 do-it-all management style was responsible for that success. Yet, he was feeling burned out, and while he worked from home he hardly interacted with his family. He could see it starting to take a toll on his marriage and in this relationship with his children. Even though he'd tried a few things to fix his situation, they hadn't helped much, and he had gotten to a stress point that he was no longer willing to tolerate. As we started working together, it became apparent that Carlos's previous attempts to pull back from his business and spend more time with his family had failed because he worried his business would fall apart if he took his eye off it even briefly. There was some resistance as we strategized small experimental steps to step away here and there from his work, but as we implemented some new systems and habits to make sure things didn't fall through the cracks, Carlos made tremendous progress. Within three months, while his business continued to plug along at slightly increased pace, and while he developed some passive income streams, Carlos spent a number of evenings every week – plus most of each weekend – with his family, getting together with friends at least once each week, and helping his wife around the house more. He also felt much more comfortable knowing that his business could continue to thrive without his relentless attention, and was more relaxed about being able to balance his home and work roles.

What you believe influences how successful you'll be because you just won't expend as much effort if you think the chances for success are slim.

Don't Say Yes to Yourself or Anyone Else if You Don't Mean It

Don't lie to yourself by saying yes if you're not dedicated or at least sincere about following through. Do you have a pet project like building something, or writing a book, or getting involved in some hobby? Don't do it, not unless you sense a really sustainable commitment, or at least enough of one to carry you through to your satisfaction. If you don't have that "juice" for it over a longer haul it will just haunt and nag at you and reduce your faith in yourself. It'll probably cost you money, too!

Mary Ellen had been meaning to start a business newsletter that she'd send out to her clients each month. She created an outline, and had ideas for articles, but had been putting off writing a series of articles for six to eight months.

As a result, Mary Ellen felt frazzled, bad, incapable, and like a fraud in her industry. When I asked why she wanted to start the newsletter, she replied that it was only good business, and that it had been suggested by someone she trusted. But Mary Ellen wasn't that interested in the newsletter beyond its supposed benefits.

By putting off the initiative, she wasn't losing anything she already had, she simply wasn't gaining what she thought would be useful. The crucial point came when I inquired about the health of her business, which she said was very good. Since business was very good and she was doing well, she had no real need to take extra action – in the form of a newsletter to improve it.

Spending eight percent of her time on the top twenty percent of her most important efforts was smarter and more vital to her business than spending eighty percent of her time on her twenty percent least important efforts. The newsletter initiative didn't make it into the top twenty percent. If, in the twenty percent of her remaining time, she decided the newsletter was worthy, she could type up a number of articles that could be used in future newsletters. For now, though, she had been beating herself up for putting off something that was unnecessary as well as not particularly enjoyable.

Graciously Saying "No" to Requests

If someone asks you for a favor your automatic reaction may be to say yes just because you don't want to disappoint them or have them dislike you. But if you don't really mean "yes", you may delay in starting on or finishing the favor, and then you really will disappoint them or give them cause to dislike you. You'll hate yourself for agreeing to it, and you'll resent the favor or the person you're doing it for, which muddies your relationship with them. If you even suspect that you won't really follow through, don't take on favors, obligations, or volunteer positions. Those offers may make you feel good or massage your ego because it's nice to be recognized, needed, and appreciated. Don't say yes, and don't worry about sounding selfish or mean.

There are ways to say no that are gracious, diplomatic, and helpful, such as, "I'm flattered you asked me, and I appreciated your faith in me" or "I wouldn't want to disappoint you by doing anything less than a fantastic job. Right now, though, my plate is too full, and I can't help you with it. Who else might be able to?"

Remember, you don't have to explain yourself or apologize, and you don't need to solve their problem for them. I'll repeat that: you don't need to solve their problem for them! If you give them the impression that you'd love to help them when you really wouldn't, they may ask you again later, so don't say things you don't mean. You'll get more comfortable at this with practice.

Leslie lived in the upstairs of a two-story house, and her mother lived downstairs. Her mom always wanted her company, and Leslie felt the same way, except that Leslie was also pursuing her own musical career, and needed to spend time and effort on it. That ate into the amount of time she could hang out with her mom. Leslie was a real "people pleaser" and she had a hard time saying no to her mother's plans for dinner and TV together, or to go shopping, or whatever else her mom felt like doing. While her mom wanted Leslie to be happy, and encouraged her to go for auditions, she didn't take Leslie's music career aspirations seriously, and would sometimes belittle Leslie's efforts. It was starting to put a strain on their relationship.

It took some wordsmithing to get the language right, as well as some patience and courage, but within a few weeks, Leslie was successful at setting some loving but firm boundaries with her mom.

Like Leslie, you may experience resistance when you start saying no, but don't let that stop you. When family and friends have known you for years, probably much longer, they expect you to behave in a certain way. Changing your behavior can make them feel a little threatened, and that's normal. Have a plan in place to get support while this is happening. Continue to use respect and kindness as criteria for saying no, and stop saying yes.

Don't Say Yes Without a Strategy

Don't say yes and neglect or forget to plan how you'll accomplish your goal (very typical for The Unplanned Procrastinator Profile). You think, "I'll get to it later," but later never seems to come. There is always something seemingly more pressing or some detail needing your immediate attention. The end of the day comes, and you haven't accomplished what you told yourself you would. You promise yourself you'll do it tomorrow, but when tomorrow comes different details get in your way, with the same result (or more likely, lack of it). Not only do you not accomplish the task, but you also end up feeling crappy about yourself. This is extremely common. If you fit the profile of Unplanned Procrastinator, Awakening Procrastinator, or Overwhelmed Procrastinator, you can really identify with that can't you?

Ironically, it's a pretty short leap from a knee-jerk yes to a well-executed and finished task. Usually, all it takes are the use of a calendar, a reminder system, and a fitting reward and consequence plan. Sounds like a lot, you say? It takes less than a minute to use. Is it worth a minute to make sure you get your task done? I'm guessing it is, or you wouldn't be reading this.

My clients find that they can accomplish 50-100% more than they used to by following a few simple steps. First, they move tasks from their to-do list onto their calendar, scheduling a dedicated date and time slot. Next, they use their voicemail, computer reminder system, or even an alarm clock as a back-up to help them remember they've committed themselves to the task at that time. Finally, they employ friends, co-workers, or family to help hold them accountable to following through.

You may have tried this kind of system in the past and found it worked for a while and then stopped working. If you're a Pushback Procrastinator, you probably felt like you were playing a game with yourself and it was silly or useless, or you felt too smart for such simple or childish approaches. In that case, the rebellious child in you has found a loophole, and you're taking advantage of it.

It's funny, because while your reaction feels like that of a mature adult, it's really a guise for self-indulgent behavior, laced with a sense of frustration. The bottom line is that you're engaged in a defensive posture and it's backfiring. While it has felt good for a while to continue finding excuses for putting things off, it eventually becomes tiresome and annoying. Try taking the word "but" out of your vocabulary. Every time you find yourself coming up with a reason why some option is not possible, instead put your efforts into looking for how it, or some other option, *could be* possible.

Maybe you're an Almost Anticrastinator, and you've tried various methods, none of which seem very effective or sustainable. It's likely that you just need more tweaking of those methods, something more appropriately tailored to your individual personality and the particular task involved. Also essential is a sense of play and willingness to experiment. Almost Anticrastinators, like Fabulous-At-Following-Through Anticrastinators, often get mired in perfectionism, which leads to rigid over-seriousness. Have some fun with this!

Over time, many strategies need continual fine-tuning and upgrading. That's just life, and it's an excellent way to stay adaptable and prepared for the inevitable changes and challenges you'll definitely face ahead. When previously effective methods stop working, it doesn't mean they were useless, it just means they can be improved for the current situation.

Putting Strategy Number Four to Work

List the goals, projects, and tasks that you say you want to do, but haven't thought about the next steps or made any plans to follow through with:

_____

_____

_____

List the goals, projects, or tasks you've given yourself that, when closely examined, you realize you're really not that interested in or committed to.

_____

_____

_____

Of all your responsibilities, obligations, and volunteer positions, which one or two is it time to move on from?

_____

_____

_____

What expectations do you have of yourself, and what expectations do others have of you, that you can now identify as unnecessary, unreasonable, out-dated, or inappropriate?

_____

_____

_____

What would you love to do (and aren't), but now know you're simply not ready for, or the timing is not right to follow through with?

_____

_____

_____

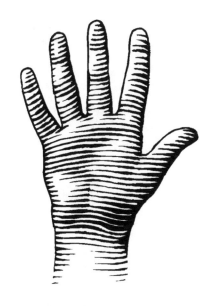

Strategy 5:

Stop Trying to Finish

Strategy 5:

Stop Trying to Finish

The truth is, finishing is overrated, at least when you're trying to get something done.

"What?!" you say? That doesn't make sense. I know it seems like I'm contradicting myself, but take a leap of faith for the moment, suspend your judgment while you read this strategy, and then see what you think once you've given it a fair trial.

The results of my Procrastination Survey, taken by hundreds of people, show that two of the most common objectives that people are doing their best to avoid are getting organized (papers, files, clutter) and writing projects (for work, educational requirements, or hobby). I have a lot of experience coaching people in these particular areas, as well as lots of other procrastination bugaboos, and one thing that's always present is the overriding focus on being done with it.

Well, of *course* you want to be done with it! But by making the end-goal your focus, you can, and do, easily get overwhelmed. The weight and dread of the seemingly monumental effort and time, not to mention tedium or difficulty, are unpleasant. In the moment, you don't recognize what this does to your concentration. Since it's an uncomfortable place to go, your attention suddenly skips light years away to some other thought or action that's a lot less distasteful. The next thing you know, instead of sorting through your piles or opening the document you're supposed to be working on, you're in front of the television, the refrigerator, the email inbox, or some other favorite procrastination location.

When your eyes are trained only on the finish line, it can seem really far away. It feels like you'll never get there, or it will be a long, painful slog to reach it. You see the obstacles that are ahead, or you worry about the barriers that might be there, before you're anywhere near them. Being prepared for complications is a good thing, but when anticipating them stops you in your tracks, you're not exactly planning your course. You're just stuck. This is familiar territory for those of you who are Procrastination Profile E people.

We're taught there's only value when we complete something. There's little appreciation or recognition in the interim for the toil we've expended, the learning we've experienced, or the initiative we've embraced. We don't see how courageous and fabulous we are. All we can see is unfinished business. Because it's not done, we see it as representing failure, our failure. And it's not just that we have failed in this one thing, but we think it implies that we are weak, lazy, and stupid, too, and it calls up so many of our previous failures, confirming that we are indeed, useless and incompetent.

Oh, happy day.

It cost Gabby happiness, as well as a good deal of self-confidence. Gabby felt like a failure, and had for some time. She contacted me because she was tired of feeling unhappy with herself and wanted to make some positive changes. So far, what she'd tried on her own hadn't given her the results she was looking for.

Gabby was typical of many of my clients and workshop participants in that she was intelligent, had a lot of interests, and liked to dabble in a number of projects. She enjoyed having a lively and engaged lifestyle, and she believed in serving her community through volunteering. She also believed that staying busy was admirable and that it kept her on her toes. These qualities, though, were also responsible for her procrastination.

Gabby liked politics and had accepted a fundraising role. She was also the newsletter editor for her neighborhood association, and she volunteered regularly for activities at her daughter's school. Recently, she had signed up for a sculpture class, and she was already involved in a sports training course for her son's benefit. While all of these activities were in line with her values, the tasks of each role or project weren't particularly engaging to her, so she delayed following through with some of those activities.

Now she'd fallen behind, and she felt stressed, concerned, and ineffective. To add to it, she had been considering moving her daughter to different school, and her husband had just been offered a transfer out of the country, one which would greatly enhance his career. They had thirty days to research and decide whether he would take the transfer or not.

Gabby had, until then, welcomed a number of obligations that she just didn't have the juice for, and now she was paying the price.

The first order of business was to applaud Gabby for stepping up to the plate to be an active citizen, community member, mother, and artist. The next step was to get her to complete any outstanding work for her volunteer positions, and then decide which other activities to let go of. This was hard for Gabby, as she'd been taught that she'd be a failure if she gave up something before finishing it. It was a new and appealing perspective to her that, as life is short, continuing with what you have little interest in is wasted effort, not failure. Since the sports training course hadn't turned out to be what she'd hoped for, dropping out of the course, while uncomfortable, really made sense to her. The neighborhood newsletter editor position kept her "in the know" about her community, but the actual editing wasn't much fun anymore. It was with a little hesitation, but a lot of relief, that she decided to resign in two months, at the end of her term, or sooner if she and her family moved. She also retired from her political activities – they were more demanding than her life currently allowed.

Meanwhile, Gabby had started taking two more classes in other areas of interest. This time, though, the obligations were much shorter-term, and she no longer felt obligated to continue with them if, once she'd got into the meat of the courses, she found that they didn't motivate or inspire her to action. She'd already spent the money to enroll in the courses, but that didn't mean she needed to spend additional energy if they turned out to be unsuitable for her needs.

You recall, of course, the childhood tale of the tortoise and the hare. The hare thought only of how slow the tortoise was and assuming he'd get to the finish line a whole lot faster. Figuring it was a no-brainer he'd win, he put off his effort and fell asleep. The tortoise only focused on the road immediately ahead, making steady and even progress. If the tortoise had made his only focus the finish line, he probably would never have agreed to the race.

In our fast-paced world, last minute marathon all-nighters are winked at. Slow and steady is almost a sin. Culturally, we're almost obsessed with speed, achievement, and winning. How many dozen television reality shows glorify only Number One, and make conniving and cheating almost acceptable? Victory is all, and success is reserved only for those who achieve the end-result, quickly.

With all this training, it's understandable that the glamour of the finish captures our imaginations to the exclusion of all else. We have an image in our minds that once we're rich and successful, life will be so easy and effortless.

There's a saying that goes, "Before enlightenment, chop wood and carry water. After enlightenment, chop wood and carry water."

Here's my version, which applies to the subject of finishing: "Before success, exercise, eat right, floss your teeth, and pay your taxes. After success, exercise, eat right, floss your teeth, and pay your taxes."

The Yuck Factor

Every year, at the top of the year, we find ourselves making all kinds of resolutions and hoping we have the self-discipline to follow through (for at least a few weeks!). Maybe it's clearing out the clutter, getting out of debt or saving money for retirement, or starting on that exercise program (all of the above?) When I look at these resolutions, I see a common denominator: the Yuck Factor. It's all stuff we feel we should do, we know it's good for us, and we really do want these things to come to pass, BUT...doing them involves getting past the parts of them that we find distasteful, uncomfortable, scary, mountainous, or just plain HARD!

We've evolved to the stage (especially in twenty-first century America) where we believe it's our birthright to live our lives with absolutely minimal discomfort, struggle, and stress. And for the most part, that's a good thing (hey, it's a GREAT thing!). But we'd never get anything accomplished if we were always in that comfort zone; there would be no motivation or inclination to do anything except enjoy our current state of bliss. The fact is, we need some Yuck Factor in order to live a satisfying life.

You've heard it before... stress can be good for us (until it turns to distress), but have you thought about how that applies to the things you know you need to do but put off because there's some pinch, some tension that's generated because you're resisting the Yuck Factor? While there's a whole lot to be said for going about things the struggle-free way (and I'm big on that!), there's just no way around the uneasiness and somewhat offensive nature of some of the stuff we need to deal with. No matter how rich, smart, healthy, or beautiful we are, there will always be requirements and necessities that we'd really like NOT to do.

So, sometimes the only answer (much as I hate to parrot a much-maligned multinational) is "just do it". Really. Just put that clothes-pin on your nose, roll up your sleeves, put on the figurative (or literal!) rubber gloves (or parachute!!), and jump in (or out!). Sometimes it really is only about taking some personal responsibility, accepting that there are prices we have to pay to get what we want, and reconciling ourselves with that reality. It becomes a lot easier to bear when we understand that it's just part of the package and there's no way around it.

It's amazing how the Yuck Factor has the ability to slow our normally quick, facile, and intelligent minds to a whimpering, fidgety halt. When a task involves pressure, tedium, fear, or stress, we suddenly lose our sense of capability and grind to a shuddering stand-still. Mostly, it's because we're fighting having to do this or that painful or uncomfortable thing, but the effect is to cloud our minds with uncertainty and confusion and to overwhelm us. We're in a state of indecision about how or where to start.

This is the crux of matter, the distinction between finishing and starting. With my clients, I've found that very often, they think they know what they need to do to finish, but because they've been avoiding it, they really don't understand the next steps. It's only through attentive discussion that we discover there are interim steps or tasks that need to be addressed first. Inevitably, by breaking these larger objectives down into immediate action steps, much of the sting is removed, and there is much less resistance to starting from this new point.

Over time, the slow and steady actions become easier and easier to deal with.

I used to work into the evening, suddenly run out of steam, and then fall into bed exhausted, without brushing my teeth or washing my face. I knew this wasn't a good thing, but I hadn't discovered enough of an incentive to make myself be a "good girl". If you recall Strategy Three – Hire a hit man to kill you if you don't follow through – I needed some expensive and painful dental work because I hadn't been rigorous with my hygiene, which provided the motivation to start taking better care of my teeth. I started seeing some aging of my skin, so I visited a doctor, who prescribed an expensive skin treatment program. Because I paid so much for that program, there was no way I wasn't going to use it! It's a long-term program, and it needs to be used every single night.

I still work into the evening and suddenly run out of steam. Each night I still feel the lure of my pillow. While my inner child continues to cry to be relieved of this obligation, each week that cry gets a little less insistent. Every night I focus on just starting by simply walking into the bathroom, and with each passing night the inner struggle to begin the routine fades more and more.

Replace thoughts of finishing with what the small next step is. It's so much less daunting that way. The next step is manageable, and you're more likely to take it, especially when you're not staring down a grueling slog. Once your focus is only on the next step, the entire project will feel less arduous.

Putting Strategy Number Five to Work

Pick the most important goal, task and project that seems complex and feels overwhelming.

_____

_____

_____

List all the steps you can think of, from current status to completion. You don't have to list them in order. Just write them down as you think of them. Use a separate piece of paper if you need more room.

_____

_____

_____

_____

_____

Now put the steps you listed above in approximate chronological order by numbering them. Don't get caught up in perfection; for now, just make some best guesses.

If you had to pick one next thing for this goal or task that you could do for only twenty minutes what would it be?

_____

_____

When is the soonest you can schedule this twenty minute activity into your calendar?

Date: _____ Time: _____

What do you want to say to yourself to focus only on the immediate task at hand when you find you're feeling overwhelmed by the prospect of the finish line? Examples are, "I can handle twenty minutes of this" or "Right now I don't have to do any more than this bit" or "This will be over before I know it."

_____

_____

_____

Assuming your deadline is over two weeks away, when are you going to schedule enough twenty minute increments in the next couple of weeks to make steady but manageable progress?

_____

_____

Who can you enlist to help you follow through?

_____

_____

_____

Final Thoughts

Congratulations and good work on making it to the end of this book! This book offers five radical strategies for overcoming procrastination. These strategies provide a strong foundation for re-patterning your neural pathways to replace unproductive attitudes and behaviors. I hope you, like so many other readers I've heard from, have enjoyed reading it and have started to apply some of the principles discussed.

If you're still stuck in some areas, don't fret. Since you don't have an extensive background or loads of experience in knowing which goals to pursue, what "hit men" might be most effective, or rewiring your thought patterns, it may be worth your while to use a trained and objective professional to help brainstorm, troubleshoot, and support you in making better progress.

Since changing your habits is mostly a matter of making a different choice at critical moments, improving your success rate really is under your control – even though it sometimes doesn't feel like it. The procrastination bug is rarely fatal, but it often does have significant costs. If you're aware of what those costs are, are you willing to continue to pay them? If you are, then accept that your choice, for the moment at least, is to stay the same. Stop battering your confidence with guilt and shame.

On the other hand, if those critical moments seem to slide by without your recognizing them before it's too late, and you really do want to make improvements, it's worth your while to delve further. We have some additional resources for you at **www.StopProcrastinatingNow.com**.

Has this book has given you a new perspective on overcoming procrastination? I'd love to hear from you with your feedback and experiences. I'm compiling more stories that illustrate the various methods people have used for ending their procrastination problems, to offer inspiration to others who haven't yet conquered their procrastination gremlins. Send your stories and feedback to: **kerul@newleafsystems.com**.

About the author

A recognized expert in procrastination, Kerul Kassel works with executives, professionals, and business owners to address the important actions and decisions they've been putting off. Kerul is an internationally recognized professional coach, author, speaker, and teleclass leader. She's certified through the International Coach Federation, the International Association of Coaches and other coaching organizations. Her clients are small business owners, professionals, executives, and she has worked with corporate organizations such as NASA, Sony, Hilton, and Volvo. Her expertise has been utilized and mentioned in many periodicals, and she was recently quoted in TIME magazine as a procrastination "nichepert".

Kerul can be hired for individual or group consulting and coaching, and for customized workshops. For more information, visit **www.NewLeafSystems.com**.

For information on her Procrastination Solutions Kit, visit **www.StopProcrastinatingNow.com**.

Kerul and her husband recently realized a long time dream of building an environmentally sensible house, living a bi-latitudinal lifestyle in New York and Florida, and she is on a journey of courage, training her 1750 lb. horse Goldilocks to be her partner and collaborator.

Kerul can be reached at **kerul@newleafsystems.com**.